Southern Gospel Piano

Devotion

Darrell Archer

WWW.MELBAY.COM

Preface

Dedication, loyalty, worship and faithfulness are truly the best indicators of devotion to anything or anyone. God has always been so consistent in His immeasurable love, undeniable compassion and tender care to those who have sought for and discovered Him, that their natural response can only be one of allegiance and devotion that is expressed in daily words, thoughts, and actions.

This is a collection of gospel songs that through the years have eloquently expressed the meaningful ways in which the Lord has revealed Himself to mankind. God has made Himself known not only through nature and His spirit but also in a more practical way by how Jesus approached life's everyday situations and what His example teaches us about how we can best honor Him and share our faith in Him with others.

Just a brief glance at some of the titles of the selections that are included in this book's contents will evoke memories of past commitments made on our spiritual journeys and also impress the need of loving the one who first loved us and is worthy of all our praise.

These pieces have been favorites of so many for so long and continue to inspire new generations of believers. These "down home" arrangements are presented with the hopeful expectation that they will inspire the same response in all that perform and hear these "Southern Gospel Songs of Devotion."

Table of Contents

All The Way My Savior Leads Me

Fanny J. Crosby

Robert Lowry
Arr. Darrell V. Archer

14
F
B♭
F
B♭/C
F
C
C7
18
F
F7
B♭6
B♭
mf
F
C/E
F
C7
22
F
F7/A
B♭6
B♭
F/C
B♭13
25
E♭
f

Bb/D
Eb
29
Ab
Eb/G
Eb/Bb
Bb/D
F
F 7/C
Bb
Bb7/F
mp
33
Eb
Ab
Eb/G
Cm
Bb7
Eb
Bb7/F
F m7/Eb
Db7
37
Gb
Bb+

C♭ A♭m7 C°7 G♭/D♭ D♭7 G♭ Bm/D D7/A
mf
41
G B+ C6 3 C G D7
G Am7/D D7
45
G G7
f
C6 C G D7/F♯ G C
dim.
mf

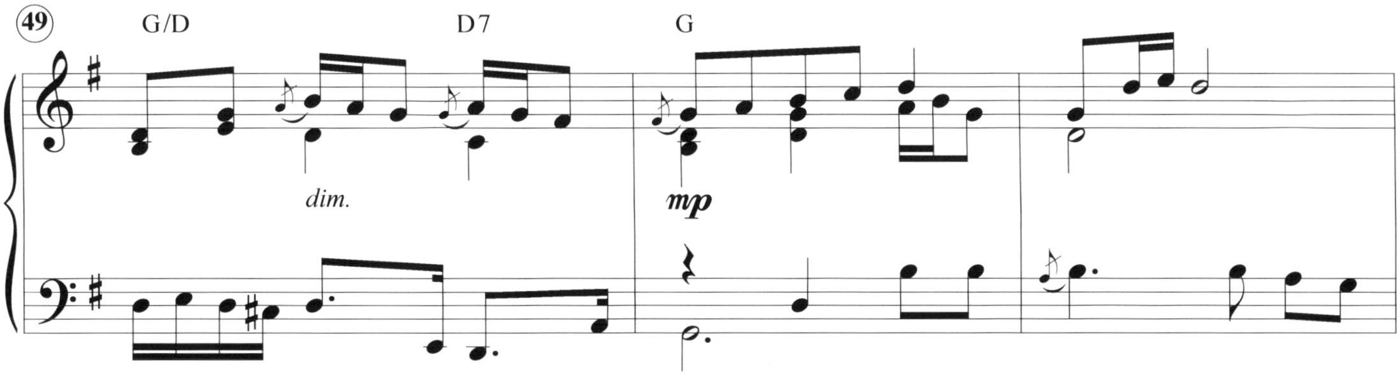

"For You are my high rock and my fortress;
For Your name's sake You will lead me and guide me."

Psalm 31:3 (LSB)

He's Everything To Me

Kate Byron

Hampton H. Sewell
Arr. Darrell V. Archer

B♭ B♭7 B♭m6 F 17 F7
B♭ 3 B♭m F/C C7/E 8va F F/C 21 F F6
f
(8va) F C7
25 (8va) Gm C7 Gm C7 F F/C

29
F
F6
F
F9/C
F7
B6
33
B♭6
B♭m6
F/C
B♭
dim.
1. F/C
C7
mf
F
8va
f
2. F/C
A7/E
A7
mf
Dm
B♭m
F/C
C7
8va
F
F/C
F
poco a poco rit. e dim.
p
8va

I Gave My Life For Thee

Philip P. Bliss
Frances R. Havergal
Arr. Darrell V. Archer

Reverently ♩. = 80

13
C
Dm
C7
F
Em
Dm
17
C/G
C/E
C
G
D7
G7
15ma
8va
C
C6
C
C/G
E♭°7
21
Dm
Dm/A
mf
(8va)
G
F/G
G7
C
C/E
C
C/G
E♭°7
mp

25 G7/D G7 G9 G7/F /E /D C C/G
15ma 8va C C/G E♭°7 29 Dm Dm7 G7
mf
(8va) C C6 C C/G E♭°7 33 G7/D G Dm6
mp
G D G7 C C/E C°7 E/B 8va E
cresc.
mf

37
even
F♯m
B7
E
poco a poco dim.
A/B E/B G°7
41 B/F♯ B D♯m/G♯ /F♯
B7 A/B B7
E
mp
3
C♯°7
45 F♯m
D7/A
B7 A/B B7
f
E
A/C♯
E
C♯°7
49 B
mp

Looking for the blessed hope
and the appearing of the glory
of our great God and Savior,
Jesus Christ,
who gave Himself for us
that He might redeem us
from all lawlessness, and purify for Himself
a people for His own possession,
zealous for good works.

Titus 2:13, 14 (LSB)

Is Your All On The Altar?

Elisha A. Hoffman
Arr. Darrell V. Archer

8va 2nd time
13
D13 D13/F♯ D7/A D13 D13/F♯ D7/F♯ G G/D C/E E♭7
8va 2nd time
G/D C/D D7
17
G D7 G C/G G D7/A
G/B G D13 D9/F♯ G G/D G
21
D13 D13/F♯ D7/A
D13 D13/F♯ D7/F♯ G G/B Dm7 G/B G7

25
C
Am
D
D7/F♯
C/G
G
Bm
mf
G7/B
Dm7
G7/B
G7
29
C
A
A6
A7
D
A7
D
5
mp
33
G
G6
D13
G
G6
G/D
G
Em7
D13
D9/F♯
G
G/D
G

37
1.
D13 D13/F♯ D7/A D13 D13/F♯ D7/F♯ G G/D C/E E♭7 G/D C/D D7
8va
41
2. D13 D13/F♯ D7/A B/D♯ B/F♯ B Em Em/B
poco a poco rit. e cresc.
A7 A9
f
mf
a tempo
45
Am9 Am7 D13 D7
G C Bm Am G
8va
rit. e dim.
mp
p

Jesus Paid It All

John T. Grape
Elvina M. Hall
Arr. Darrell V. Archer

8va
13
E♭ Fm/E♭ E♭ A♭ B♭/A♭ A♭ E♭ Gm7
Fm7 B♭7/F B♭7
17
E♭ B+ G7
A♭ A°7 C°7 E♭ Cm Fm9 B♭7
E♭ Gm7 C7 B♭/C
22
F
poco rit. e cresc.
mf
a tempo

Dm Dm7 Gm7 C7 F B♭/C
8va
26
(8va)
F A7 A7/C♯ Dm B♭m F D Gm7 C7
F Am7 D7(♭9)
30
G
Rhythm Tacet
p
cresc.

34
G F♯ G9 G7/D
B+ B7 C
G/D B B7/D♯
mf
poco a poco rit. e cresc.
Em A9 Cm Am7(♭5)
38
G F E
f
mp
Am7 D7
G C△ Bm7 Am7
G
8va
rit. e dim.
pp

O Why Not Tonight?

J. Calvin Bushey
Arr. Darrell V. Archer

Elizabeth Reed

E♭ A♭ E♭
B♭ A♭/B♭ B♭7
E♭ A♭ E♭
cresc.
15
A♭
E♭
Fm
E♭/B♭ E♭ B♭7
mf
E♭ C7
19
F F/C C7
F
mp
cresc.
mf
C7
F
23
F B♭

F
B♭
F/C
C7
F
D
C/E
/F♯
even
cresc.
27
G
G6/D
G6
D7
G/G
/E
G6/D
/B
G6/G
/B
C△
C♯°7
f
D
D6/A
D
D7/A
G
G⁹₆/D
G⁹₆
G
31
C
to CODA
G/G
/F♯
/E
/E♭
G/D
/B
C
Am7
G
G/D
D/F♯
D7

G (Tacet)
8va
35 G G/D G C
(8va)
G/G /F♯ /E /E♭ G/D C Am7 G G/D D/F♯ D7
G D C/E /F♯ 39 Em Em/B Em Am G/D D7
CODA
G C Am A♭7 G D G

Only Trust Him

John H. Stockton
Arr. Darrell V. Archer

Expressively ♩ = 70

13
F
F7
3
F7/A
B♭
F
mf
Dm
Gm7
C7
17
F
F7
3
F7/A
B♭
F
Dm
G7
C7
F
D7
3
dim.

21
G
mp
Am/G
G/B
3
G/D
G
B7/D♯
3
Em
Am
D
D7
25
G/B
G
B+
C
C/G
C
G
Em7
G/D
D7
G
G/D

29
G
G7/B
C
C/G
G
Em
mf
p
Am
D7
33
G
G7/B
C
C/G
G
mf
Em
G/D
B7/D♯
Em
A9/C♯
8va
37
G
Em
p
poco a poco rit. e cresc.
ff
mp
a tempo
Am
D7
G
G/E
G/D
G
G/D
G
rit. e dim.
p

Pass Me Not, O Gentle Saviour

W. H. Doane
Arr. Darrell V. Archer

Fanny J. Crosby

♩. = 63
A
D
A/C♯
E7/B
11
A
A7/E
D6
D
A
F♯m
Bm
E7
15
A
D
A
F♯m
Bm
A/E
E7
A
A/C♯
E7/D
C♯°/E

19
D
D7
G
D
Bm
Em7
A7
mf
D
23
F♯+
G
D
Bm
Em
F♯m
A7
D
D7
27
G
G7
f
C6
C
G
Em

Am
Am/G
F
F7
31
B♭
D+
E♭
ff
B♭
Gm
Cm
Cm7
F13
F♯°7
Gm
Gm7
C9
rit. e dim.
35
Cm7
Dm/F
F7
mp
slower tempo
B♭
E♭
B♭
E♭
B♭
E♭
B♭/D
Cm7
B♭
rit.
3

Softly and Tenderly

Will L. Thompson
Arr. Darrell V. Archer

F♯7+
G
D
17 Bm
Em
D/A
Bm
C♯°
D
D2
D
D7
21 B♭
mp
D+
D7
D+
E♭
E♭/B♭
B♭
25 Gm
Gm(△7)
Gm7
C9
E°
Cm/G
Cm
Cm/G
F
C+
F9

29
B♭
D+
D
D+
E♭
E♭/B♭
B♭
33
Gm
Cm
B♭/F
3
B♭
B♭/A
Gm7
p
37
F
Cm7/F
F
D7
Gm
F7
B♭
41
F
Gm
C
mp

F
C7
F7
G
3
G♭/B♭
rit.
(♭)
Bm7(♭5)
F/A
G9
47
C
a tempo
mf
G/D
C/E
F
F/C
C
51
Am
Dm
C/G
G7
C
dim. e rit.
F
C/E
Dm7
C
mp
p

www.melbay.com